50

THINGS TO DO BEFORE YOU'RE

11¾

National Trust

My adventure notebook
for wild times outdoors

National Trust

First published in the United Kingdom in 2015 by
National Trust Books
1 Gower Street, London WC1E 6HD

An imprint of Pavilion Books Group Ltd

© National Trust 2015
The National Trust is a registered charity, no. 205846

Designed for the National Trust by 18 feet and rising. Based on
original concept and content by Behaviour Change with design work
by N. Duncan Mills.

Photographs ©National Trust Images/Josh Cole; p. 5 National Trust
Images/Arnhel de Serra; p. 24 National Trust Images/Paul Harris; pp. 36,
60 National Trust Images/David Levenson; pp. 12, 48, 75 National Trust
Images/John Millar
Illustrations by N. Duncan Mills

The information on pp. 72–83 is based on data collected by the
National Trust between May and August 2014.

All rights reserved. No part of this publication may be reproduced,
stored in a retrieval system, or transmitted in any form or by any
means, mechanical, photocopying, recording or otherwise, without
the prior permission of the copyright owner.

ISBN: 978 1 909881 38 9

A CIP catalogue record for this book is available from
the British Library.

Printed and bound by 1010 Printing International Ltd, China

This book can be ordered direct from the publisher at
the website www.anovabooks com, or try your local
bookshop. Also available at National Trust shops and
www.nationaltrust.org.uk/shop

Contents

50 things to do before you¹re 11¾   8

Where do I begin?   9

Continue the adventure online   9

Adventurer

1. Climb a tree   14
2. Roll down a really big hill   15
3. Camp out in the wild   16
4. Build a den   17
5. Skim a stone   18
6. Run around in the rain   19
7. Fly a kite   20
8. Catch a fish with a net   21
9. Eat an apple from a tree   22
10. Play conkers   23

Discoverer

11. Go on a really long bike ride   26
12. Make a trail with sticks   27
13. Make a mud pie   28
14. Dam a stream   29
15. Play in the snow   30
16. Make a daisy chain   31
17. Set up a snail race   32
18. Create some wild art   33
19. Play pooh sticks   34
20. Jump over waves   35

Ranger

21. Pick blackberries growing in the wild — 38
22. Explore inside a tree — 39
23. Visit a farm — 40
24. Go on a walk barefoot — 41
25. Make a grass trumpet — 42
26. Hunt for fossils and bones — 43
27. Go star gazing — 44
28. Climb a huge hill — 45
29. Explore a cave — 46
30. Hold a scary beast — 47

Tracker

31. Hunt for bugs — 50
32. Find some frogspawn — 51
33. Catch a falling leaf — 52
34. Track wild animals — 53
35. Discover what's in a pond — 54
36. Make a home for a wild animal — 55
37. Check out the crazy creatures in a rock pool — 56
38. Bring up a butterfly — 57
39. Catch a crab — 58
40. Go on a nature walk at night — 59

Explorer

41. Plant it, grow it, eat it — 62
42. Go swimming in the sea — 63
43. Build a raft — 64
44. Go bird watching — 65
45. Find your way with a map and compass — 66
46. Try rock climbing — 67
47. Cook on a campfire — 68
48. Learn to ride a horse — 69
49. Find a geocache — 70
50. Canoe down a river — 71

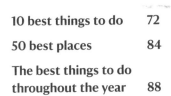

10 best things to do — 72

50 best places — 84

The best things to do throughout the year — 88

50 things to do before you're 11¾

Welcome to the great outdoors...
Crazy creatures, awesome antics, hidden
treasures! Thrills, hills, sun and fun, there's
everything you need for an excellent adventure!
With help from kids all over the country,
we've put together a list of great
challenges for you; the ultimate
50 things to do before you're
11¾, and we're making it as easy
as mud pie to do them somewhere
near you with a little helping hand
from the National Trust.

Caution: Some
of them may
cause extreme
excitement.

Note to grown-ups: Children matter to the
National Trust, so we recommend that all these
activities are supervised by an adult. We trust
that you will make your own judgement about
what is safe and suitable for the ability of your
child. Just remember to have fun!

Where do I begin?

Your adventure notebook will take you into the woods and onto the water, up huge hills and down to the beach. Plus there are plenty of ways to make the most of what's closer to home. At the National Trust we have all the space you'll need; we don't mind if you make some noise or get mucky, so long as you always have a grown-up with you to make sure you're still in one piece by the time you're 11¾.

This book consists of 5 sections of 10 activities, each getting more adventurous as you go through.

You can continue your adventures on the 50 things website – 50things.org.uk – or by downloading our free 50 things app. The website offers hints and tips to help you complete all of your 50 things and the chance to unlock some secret rewards as you tick the things off! You can also find which of our National Trust places are near to you and the activities you can do there. Then rate your favourite activities and upload photographs of you doing them to really complete your record of achievements.

Now you can tick off your completed activities while out and about! Try our new free 50 things app, available on iOS from iTunes App Store and Android from the Google Play store.

And you can join in online at
nationaltrust.org.uk/50things

'You get to run around and learn to do something new.'

Recommended by Amelie, aged 3

Adventurer

Tick off each activity as you complete it.

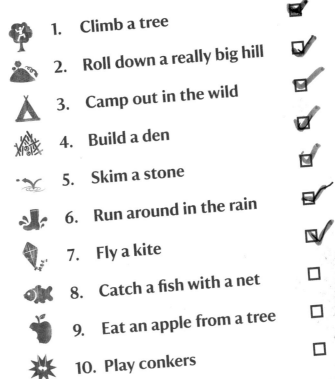

1. Climb a tree ☑
2. Roll down a really big hill ☑
3. Camp out in the wild ☑
4. Build a den ☑
5. Skim a stone ☑
6. Run around in the rain ☑
7. Fly a kite ☑
8. Catch a fish with a net ☐
9. Eat an apple from a tree ☐
10. Play conkers ☐

1. Climb a tree

Check out the view!

What you need:

- A tree with big strong branches you can reach from the ground
- Trainers or boots - you don't want splinters in your toes
- A big wave for everyone down below

See if you can collect some leaves on the way down and stick one on this page:

TOP TIP

Keep three of your arms and legs on the tree at all times, and always be sure to never forget to check it's dry before you climb.

Find out what kind of tree you climbed and write it here:

Date completed: Day _____ Month _____ Year _____

2. Roll down a really big hill

It's the fun way to get to the bottom.

What you need:

- A grassy hill
- A clear run with nothing you might bump into

Rolling down the hill makes you feel all dizzy and swirly. Can you draw an impression of yourself here after you've finished rolling?

TOP TIP

A fun roll is a fast roll. To really pick up speed lie on the grass, make your body into the shape of a sausage and roll down the hill sideways. Watch out for poo from animals like sheep, as it can spread nasty germs.

How many times did you roll over? Write it here:

Date completed: Day _____ Month _____ Year _____

3. Camp out in the wild

Why sleep in a boring bed when you can sleep
outside like a cowboy?

What you need:

- Go back to basics with a tent,
  ground mat and sleeping bag...or
  you can make yourself really cosy
  by taking your favourite pillow,
  duvet and a blow-up mattress
- Everyone needs a torch when
  they're camping out

What nature sounds did
you hear in the night?

Can you draw a picture of one
of the animals that you heard?

TOP TIP

Before setting up your
tent, pick a nice flat open
area and clear away any
stones or branches that
might wake you up if you
roll on them.

Keep an eye
out for bats, moths
and owls which only
come out at night

Date completed: Day _____ Month _____ Year _____

4. Build a den

Branches, twigs and leaves make surprisingly cosy dens.

What you need:

- Branches, twigs, leaves and mud, all of which are generously provided by nature for free
- Leave the power tools at home, you won't need them here

Take a photo of you in your den and stick it here:

TOP TIP

Choose a dry flat spot for the most solid den and never build with sharp objects. It could help to start by leaning sticks against a low tree branch like a wig-wam.

Date completed: Day _____ Month _____ Year _____

5. Skim a stone

Can you do four bounces?

What you need:

- Flat water, like a pond, lake or the sea on a calm day
- Somewhere to stand where you won't fall in when you throw really hard
- Some flat stones from near the water's edge

TOP TIP

Choose your stone carefully: the smoother, rounder and flatter the better. Throw it hard and low so it spins quickly across the top of the water. Make sure there's nothing in the water you might hit, like ducks or swimmers!

Not all water ripples are made from skimming stones. Sometimes they are made from things under the water. Can you draw something else you've seen that makes water ripple?

How many bounces did your stone make? Write it here:

Date completed: Day _____ Month _____ Year _____

6. Run around in the rain

Time to make a splash!

What you need:

- A rainy day
- Welly boots
- A raincoat
- Or a towel and a change of clothes

Some animals love getting wet. Make a list of animals you think are happy when it rains and draw a picture of your favourite one here:

TOP TIP

Getting wet in the rain is fun if you know you can get dry again afterwards. If you don't have a raincoat, dry off with a towel and change into some dry clothes.

Date completed: Day _____ Month _____ Year _____

7. Fly a kite

A windy day is a perfect day for flying a kite.

What you need:

- Plenty of wind
- A wide open space
- A kite!

Can you design a colourful pattern on the kite below?

TOP TIP

For your kite to really fly, it needs a nice clear sky and a large open space – don't forget to look up and check nothing will get in the way before you begin to fly!

Find out more about how to make your own kite at 50things.org.uk.

Date completed: Day _____ Month _____ Year _____

8. Catch a fish with a net

You have to be quick to catch a fish!

What you need:

- Somewhere fish live (the sea, a river, a canal or a lake)
- Somewhere you can stand or sit for a while safely
- A net
- Permission from the person who owns the land

Draw a picture of your fish and give it a name.

TOP TIP

Fishing takes time and patience: find someone who knows all about fishing to help you catch a whopper. Don't forget that fish like where they live and want to stay there. Always put them quickly and carefully back into the water. For more help and advice visit the 50 things website.

Look carefully to see if you've caught any little fish such as sticklebacks and minnows which are found in streams

What fish did you catch?

Date completed: Day _____ Month _____ Year _____

9. Eat an apple straight from a tree

Money doesn't grow on trees but apples do!

What you need:

- An apple tree – with eating apples
- Somebody to help you reach the branches
- Permission from whoever owns the tree

There are more than 700 different types of apples in the UK. What is the name of the one you picked and what colour was it?

TOP TIP

The ripest apples are on the outside branches of the tree, furthest away from the trunk. Don't eat raw cooking apples – they could give you a bad tummy ache.

Nibbles the caterpillar lives in this apple.

See if you can turn it into a nice cosy home for him:

Date completed: Day _____ Month _____ Year _____

10. Play conkers

It's not always the biggest conker that wins!

What you need:

- A conker
- Some string
- A worthy opponent
- A grown-up to help you get the string through the conker

In the template below, can you design some war paint for your conker to go into battle with? Why not try painting it onto your real conker. And you could give it a name and write it here too.

TOP TIP

To choose a killer conker, put some conkers in a bucket of water; all those that sink to the bottom are winners, those that float are losers. Ask your Mum or Dad to teach you how to play. If they can't remember (it's a while since they were kids!) you can check out the details on the 50 things website.

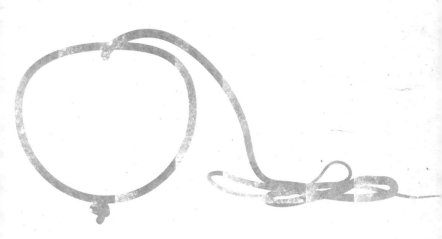

Date completed: Day _____ Month _____ Year _____

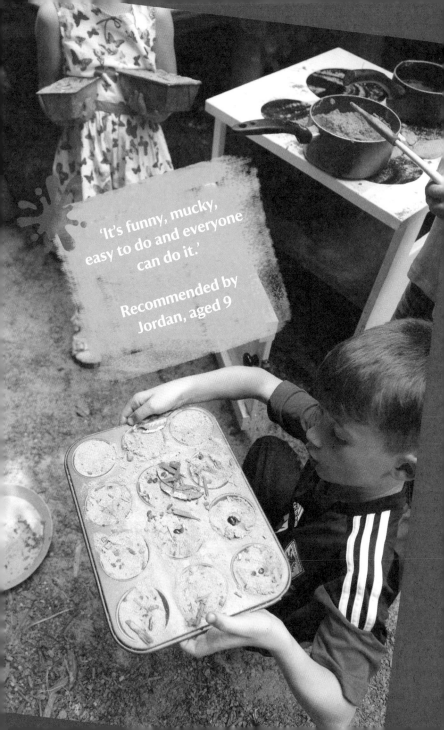

'It's funny, mucky, easy to do and everyone can do it.'

Recommended by Jordan, aged 9

Discoverer

Tick off each activity as you complete it.

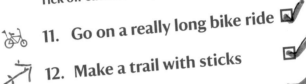 11. Go on a really long bike ride ✓

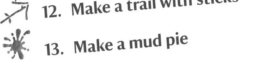 12. Make a trail with sticks ✓

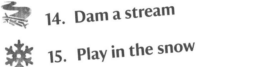 13. Make a mud pie ✓

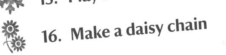 14. Dam a stream ☐

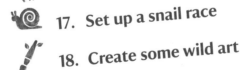 15. Play in the snow ✓

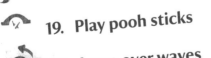 16. Make a daisy chain ✓

17. Set up a snail race ☐

18. Create some wild art ✓

19. Play pooh sticks ✓

20. Jump over waves ✓

11. Go on a really long bike ride

The speedy way to explore the great outdoors.

What you need:

- A bike which is in good working order
- A bike helmet
- A grown-up to accompany
  you on your biking adventure

TOP TIP

Take a map with you,
so you know where
you're going!

Draw a map of your bike ride below so you can
show your friends exactly where you went:

Date completed: Day _____ Month _____ Year _____

12. Make a trail with sticks

Use sticks as arrows and mark a path through the woods.

What you need:

- Lots of straight sticks to lay on the ground in the shape of arrows so they're really clear for your friends and family to follow

Draw or stick a picture of you all at the end of your trail here:

TOP TIP

You can make the trail really good fun by going over logs and around trees, and bring something fun to hide as a treasure at the end of it.

How many sticks did you use to make your trail? Write it here:

Date completed: Day _____ Month _____ Year _____

13. Make a mud pie

Recipe: Mud. More mud.

What you need:

- Lots of mud
- Stones and leaves for decorating your pie
- Optional extras include bucket, spade, water and sticks to help you move the mud around

TOP TIP

Mud pies might look delicious but they don't taste great, so never eat a mud pie. Don't forget to wash your hands afterwards.

Oozy sticky mud makes great finger prints. Can you and your friends or family all make a thumbprint in the space below to remember your day? You could even turn them into little thumb people.

Worms and lots of tiny animals actually live in mud, look out for them!

Date completed: Day _____ Month _____ Year _____

28

14. Dam a stream

It won't be long before the stream's a pond!

What you need:

- Twigs
- Branches
- Stones
- Rocks

What kind of animals do you think live near the river bank? Draw them here:

TOP TIP

What goes up must come down – you can have fun smashing down the dam once you've made it but don't go in too deep.

Date completed: Day _____ Month _____ Year _____

15. Play in the snow

Keep your fingers cosy and your toes toasty.

What you need:

- Lots of clean white snow
- Waterproof clothes and layers to keep you warm and dry

Ask someone to take a photo of you and your snow creation and stick it below:

TOP TIP

If you've made a snowman before then why not try making a snow sculpture of your favourite animal?

Give it a name and write it here:

Date completed: Day _____ Month _____ Year _____

16. Make a daisy chain

A perfect gift for the fairies.

What you need:

– Daisies

You can stick your daisy chain here when it's done or just one daisy if you have a long chain:

TOP TIP

Try to find daisies with long, thick stems to use to make the chain. They will be easier to make holes in and they won't break easily.

How many daisies did you use to make your chain?

Daisies don't really mind being picked as it makes them grow more flowers

Date completed: Day _____ Month _____ Year _____

17. Set up a snail race

On your marks, get set, go...slowly!

What you need:

– Some snails
– A circle of chalk to mark your finish line
– Team colours for your snails (stickers work well)

A snail's shell is its home and helps protect it from harm. Draw a picture of its spiralled shape and markings:

REMEMBER:

Snails are slow movers so don't make the track too long! Keep them cool and wet so they have the best chance of winning. Make sure you put them back where you found them.

Write the name of the snail that came 1st here:

Date completed: Day _____ Month _____ Year _____

18. Create some wild art

Set your creativity free!

What you need:

- A collection of leaves, twigs, feathers and seed pods
- Some paper, some glue
- A flat, dry surface to work on in a sheltered spot

Your picture or sculpture will likely be too big to include here, but you can take a photo of it and stick it in here or make a smaller picture with leftover leaves and feathers:

TOP TIP

Try to find materials that vary in colour and texture so you have lots of choice and can make something really interesting and individual.

Date completed: Day _____ Month _____ Year _____

19. Play pooh sticks

Get your sticks at the ready!

What you need:

- A good-sized stick and one you'll recognise (so you'll know who won!)
- A bridge with nicely flowing water running under it. But you must be careful of traffic if the bridge you're standing on is also a road

Which sticks, big, small, thick or thin won the most?

TOP TIP

Why not decorate your stick by tying a leaf or some grass to it so you know exactly which one is yours when it comes out from the other side of the bridge?

Write who came in 1st, 2nd and 3rd place here:

1st.

2nd.

3rd.

Date completed: Day _____ Month _____ Year _____

20. Jump over waves

Big, small, blue or green, all waves are great to jump over!

What you need:

– A spot where you know the depth of water you are entering before you start to make sure you don't go in too deep
– A grown-up to jump with you

What other animals can you think of that would be good at jumping over waves? Can you draw one of them jumping over the waves below?

TOP TIP

Watch out for underwater rocks or crevices which might hurt you, when picking your jumping spot.

Date completed: Day _____ Month _____ Year _____

'It gives you a chance to hold it and not be frightened.'

Recommended by Lucy, aged 10

Ranger

Tick off each activity as you complete it.

 21. **Pick blackberries growing in the wild**

 22. **Explore inside a tree**

 23. **Visit a farm**

 24. **Go on a walk barefoot**

 25. **Make a grass trumpet**

 26. **Hunt for fossils and bones**

 27. **Go star gazing**

 28. **Climb a huge hill**

 29. **Explore a cave**

 30. **Hold a scary beast**

21. Pick blackberries growing in the wild

They're not just tasty treats, they make great drawing tools too.

What you need:

- Bushes full of blackberries
- A stick to lift branches while you pick to avoid getting spiked by thorns
- Help from a grown-up who knows what they're doing

Can you draw a picture with your fingers just using blackberry juice?

TOP TIP

September is a prime time to pick blackberries from hedgerows – they're everywhere! Remember to wash your blackberries before eating as they've been out in the wild and don't forget to leave some for the birds!

Date completed: Day _____ Month _____ Year _____

22. Explore inside a tree

Some trees have hollows so big you can climb right inside.

What you need:

– A tree with a big hole in it

– A magnifying glass to look for mini-beasts

– A torch to look deep into the holes

Use some coloured crayons to take a rubbing of the tree that you climbed into. Cut out a piece of your rubbing and stick it here:

TOP TIP

The oldest trees have the biggest hollows, so look for the big tall trees.

Lots of insects live inside hollow trees, like beetles, eating the rotting wood. Look closely and you'll see their burrowing holes

Date completed: Day _____ Month _____ Year _____

23. Visit a farm

**One of the best places to get up close and
personal with new furry friends.**

What you need:

- A farm you can visit with
  experts who can tell you all
  about the animals

Draw a picture of your favourite
animal and write down what you
learnt about it today:

TOP TIP

Make sure that after your
farm visit, you wash your
hands really well before
you eat or drink anything.

Keep an eye out
for birds too!
Barns are good for
spotting swallows
and hedgerows are
great for seeing
robins

Date completed: Day _____ Month _____ Year _____

24. Go on a walk barefoot

You'll never want to put your shoes back on when you feel the tickly grass between your toes.

What you need:

- A towel to clean your feet with before you put your socks back on

Draw a picture of your footprints below. If your feet get muddy enough you could even make a toe print!

TOP TIP

Keep your eyes open for glass or other things that might poke you. Ouch!

25. Make a grass trumpet

Blow into a blade of grass and start up the band.

What you need:

– A clean, wide blade of grass
– A big breath
– 2 hands

Are there any other things from nature that you could use as a musical instrument?

TOP TIP

For the loudest squeak, make a hole in the grass with your fingernail and then position the grass right in between your thumbs and press your lips firmly together before you blow.

Stick your grass trumpet here:

Date completed: Day _____ Month _____ Year _____

26. Hunt for fossils and bones

There aren't many dinosaur bones around these days but you never know what other treasure you might find if you dig around.

What you need:

– A bucket and spade

– A grown-up to go searching with you

Draw a picture of the creature you think your bones or fossils might have come from:

TOP TIP

Dogs are known for burying their bones and anything else that they can lay their paws on. When you're digging around, make sure you're not digging up what a dog has left behind.

Make sure you know The Fossil Code:

1. Stay away from cliffs

2. Don't hammer or dig in cliffs

3. Keep away from cliff edges

4. Always go collecting when the tide is going out

5. Be aware of weather conditions

6. You can collect things which have been naturally unearthed or washed up, but don't dig up stuff where it was originally buried

7. Take a grown-up with you

Date completed: Day _____ Month _____ Year _____

27. Go star gazing

If you're lucky you might be able to make a wish on a shooting star!

What you need:

– A clear night with few clouds

– A place with no street lights

– A grown-up to go with you to star gaze

If you could name a star, what would you call it?

TOP TIP

Orion's Belt is one of the easiest constellations to spot and is in the night sky during the winter months. Just look for 3 bright stars in a straight line.

What other constellations did you see? Draw the brightest one here:

Date completed: Day _____ Month _____ Year _____

28. Climb a huge hill

Go to the top and touch the sky.

What you need:

- A huge hill
- A footpath to take you to the top
- Trainers or boots – leave your flip-flops behind

Stick in a photo of the view from the top of the hill or draw what you saw:

TOP TIP

If the hill is really huge, walking up might seem like hard work at times, but don't forget there's nothing better than a sing-song to keep spirits up. And remember, stay away from drops and edges.

Date completed: Day _____ Month _____ Year _____

29. Explore a cave

Don't forget your torch – you're going to need it!

What you need:

- Trainers or shoes that will grip as caves can be slippery
- A torch so you can see
- An adult to explore with you. Even experts never enter a cave alone

Close your eyes and see if you can draw a picture of yourself without looking – just like you're in a dark, dark cave:

TOP TIP

Have fun but do be careful not to disturb any wildlife living in the cave.

Special species live in caves, such as cave spiders and glow-in-the-dark mosses

Date completed: Day _____ Month _____ Year _____

30. Hold a scary beast

It might be scary at the time but think how brave you'll feel after.

What you need:

– A scary animal, perhaps a scurrying spider, a slimy slug or a big beetle (avoid things that may sting or bite)

Draw the scariest beast you can think of:

TOP TIP

They may look tough, but make sure you handle your scary beast with care.

What scary beast did you hold? Write it here:

Date completed: Day _____ Month _____ Year _____

'If you go pond-dipping you can find little animals like newts.'

Recommended by Emma, aged 8

Tracker

Tick off each activity as you complete it.

 31. **Hunt for bugs**

 32. **Find some frogspawn**

 33. **Catch a falling leaf**

 34. **Track wild animals** ☐

 35. **Discover what's in a pond**

 36. **Make a home for a wild animal**

 37. **Check out the crazy creatures in a rock pool**

 38. **Bring up a butterfly**

 39. **Catch a crab**

 40. **Go on a nature walk at night** ☐

31. Hunt for bugs

What's the creepiest crawly you can find?

What you need:

– Places where bugs like to hide, such as under rocks, in the mud or the bark of fallen trees

Draw the best bug you found:

TOP TIP

Remember, you're a giant compared to these little beasts so be gentle – take a look before you touch. You might be having too much fun to want to go home but bugs like where they live so make sure you put them back.

If your bug could talk, what would it say to you?

Date completed: Day _____ Month _____ Year _____

32. Find some frogspawn

**You think frogspawn looks weird?
Just wait until they become tadpoles!**

What you need:

- A bucket or a plastic tub
- A net to scoop them out
- A grown-up to supervise while you scoop
- Somewhere you can stand or sit safely

Can you draw what you think the frogspawn might look like when it's halfway to being a frog? You'll have to go back in a few weeks to see if you're right!

TOP TIP

Spring is the best time to find frogspawn but don't take the frogspawn away – they're happy in their home. Once you've had a look, put them back in the pond.

A frog can lay around 5,000 eggs at once that can take over a month to turn to tadpoles!

Date completed: Day _____ Month _____ Year _____

33. Catch a falling leaf

It's harder than you think.

What you need:

– A tree with lots of big leaves

Stick your favourite leaf on this page.

Why is this your favourite?

> **TOP TIP**
>
> Leaves start to fall off trees in autumn, so it's the best time of year to try catching them. If it's a windy day, stand so the wind blows into you – it will help bring the leaves towards you.

What type of tree does the leaf come from?'

Date completed: Day _____ Month _____ Year _____

34. Track wild animals

Animals are easy to find if you follow their footprints, feathers, fur and poo.

What you need:

- Sharp eyes
- Trainers or boots so you can track down animals wherever they roam

Draw a picture of the footprints you find on this page.

What animal do you think they come from?

> ### TOP TIP
>
> Remember, animals don't wear shoes so their footprints don't all look the same. From a horse's hoof to a rabbit's paw, learn what you're looking for. Whatever you do, don't touch the poo!

How many tracks did you come across? Write the number here:

35. Discover what's in a pond

Murky pond water is full of life. Scoop some out into a tub and check out what lurks beneath.

What you need:

- A clean, empty plastic tub
- A fine net
- Somewhere you can stand or sit safely
- A grown-up to go with you

Draw what you found at the bottom of your net:

TOP TIP

Scoop the net 3 times in a figure-of-eight to pick up the littlest creatures and empty the contents into the tub. If you don't spot anything at first, take a closer look. Pond life tends to be quite tiny. Remember to return the mini-beasts to their homes.

Date completed: Day _____ Month _____ Year _____

36. Make a home for a wild animal

It's not just dogs, cats, hamsters and fish that need homes.

What you need:

- Bits and pieces that you will have in the garden, such as moss, twigs or stones
- String or glue to help fasten it all together
- A flat, dry and sheltered surface to work on

What kind of animals moved into your home?

How long did they stay for?

TOP TIP

All sorts of animals need homes. You could try making a bug hotel, hedgehog house or even a bird box. Once it's completed, think about the best place to put it. Some animals prefer sunshine while others like shade.

Date completed: Day _____ Month _____ Year _____

37. Check out the crazy creatures in a rock pool

What's the weirdest looking thing you can find?

What you need:

- A clean plastic tub or bucket to scoop the water out
- A small net to help you catch things
- A low tide

What's the weirdest thing you found in the rock pool?

Can you draw it here?

TOP TIP

Keep your hands out of the pool or you might feel a little nibble or pinch! These crazy creatures like where they live, so don't forget to put them back afterwards.

Starfish can push their stomachs out of their mouths so they can gobble up and digest anything that's too big to swallow!

Date completed: Day _____ Month _____ Year _____

38. Bring up a butterfly

**Once a caterpillar makes its chrysalis, it may become
a beautiful butterfly in less than six weeks.**

What you need:

- A caterpillar
- A large plastic tub with small holes in the lid
- Leaves from one of the caterpillar's favourite plants
- Slightly damp soil or sand to line the bottom of the tub
- A twig or two to lean against the side of the tub

TOP TIP

Avoid hairy caterpillars as some of them can sting. Visit our website for more advice on how to choose and look after your caterpillar.

Draw a picture of how your caterpillar looks each week so you can show how it's changed:

Week 1

Week 2

Week 3

Week 4

Week 5

Week 6

Date completed: Day _____ Month _____ Year _____

39. Catch a crab

With the right bait and a piece of string it's easier than you might think.

What you need:

- String or crab line
- A good spot by the sea to get settled
- Scraps of bacon or fish for the bait
- A bucket of water if you'd like to take a closer look before they go back in

Count up all the legs and claws on the crab you catch and make a sketch of what it looks like:

TOP TIP

Tie the stone and bait to the end of the string so it sinks properly. When you feel it tugging, pull the string up at a good pace – too fast and the crab will fall off, too slowly and it will eat all the bait. Be careful when picking up crabs (they're not afraid to use those pincers) and put them back in the water afterwards.

40. Go on a nature walk at night

Some creatures only come out at night so this is the only chance you've got of spotting them!

What you need:

- A torch
- A grown-up who can show you where to look
- Trainers or boots – leave your slippers at home!
- Warm clothing (pyjamas don't count!)

Switch off your torch and stand silently for 5 minutes to fully experience how life is for animals in the dark.

Write what you heard below:

TOP TIP

Only use your torch when you really need to. These animals aren't afraid of the dark. They are afraid of noisy humans though, so be as quiet as a mouse.

Date completed: Day _____ Month _____ Year _____

'It is a really fun activity and adults can join in too.'

Recommended by Ben, aged 11

Explorer

Tick off each activity as you complete it.

 41. Plant it, grow it, eat it ✓

 42. Go swimming in the sea ✓

 43. Build a raft ☐

 44. Go bird watching ☐

 45. Find your way with a map and compass ☐

 46. Try rock climbing ✓

 47. Cook on a campfire ✓

 48. Learn to ride a horse ✓

 49. Find a geocache ☐

 50. Canoe down a river ✓

Date completed: Day _____ Month _____ Year _____

61

41. Plant it, grow it, eat it

Just like you, fruit and vegetables need a bit of time to grow but they're definitely worth the wait.

What you need:

- Fruit or vegetable plants or seeds
- A pot to plant them in
- Peat-free compost

Can you draw a picture of your plant each week to show how it grows?

TOP TIP

Make sure you plant the right thing at the right time. Visit eatseasonably.co.uk for all the information you need to grow your own.

Home-grown food tastes best! Try growing different fruit or vegetables across the year and see if you agree

42. Go swimming in the sea

It's much more fun than swimming in a pool.

What you need:

- Choose a warm, sunny day
- Goggles
- An adult to swim with you
- A towel to dry-off after your swim

When you dry off from your swim, sit on the beach and look out to sea. What can you spot on the horizon?

TOP TIP

The sea can be powerful. With a grown-up, look for an area where the water is calm and not too deep.

Draw what you see in the binoculars below:

Date completed: Day _____ Month _____ Year _____

43. Build a raft

It's a pirate's life for me, just watch out for the ducks!

What you need:

- Sticks and string to tie them all together
- A pond or small stream to test your raft
- Shoes that don't matter if they get wet
- A grown-up to help you near the water

Draw a diagram of your raft below and see if your friends can follow your instructions to build their own rafts too:

TOP TIP

When launching a raft look for some calm water which isn't too deep to give the raft the best chance of launching, not sinking! If you're adventurous, join a class or event where you can build a raft big enough for you to race on.

Date completed: Day _____ Month _____ Year _____

44. Go bird watching

Keep silent as a mouse and watch the birds at play.

What you need:

- A place where birds like to fly or search for food
- A quiet spot to sit and hide while you watch the birds
- A pair of binoculars and a camera

Why not make a list of all the birds you spot so that you can compare it with other adventurers?

TOP TIP

Birds get frightened off very easily – stay quiet so they don't fly away before you can identify them.

Nearly 600 different types of birds have been seen in the UK!

Draw a picture or stick a photo of a bird you spot here:

Date completed: Day _____ Month _____ Year _____

45. Find your way with a map and compass

You'll never get lost if you can use these trusty tools.

What you need:

- A map
- A compass
- A destination
- A whistle to let people know where you are

Draw your own map of where you went:

TOP TIP

Always work out where you are on the map before you even set off so you know you're starting in the right place. It also helps if you hold the map the right way round!

Date completed: Day _____ Month _____ Year _____

46. Try rock climbing

Keep your eyes peeled for some big cracks and places to get a good grip.

What you need:

- A rock that's stable and isn't wet or too steep
- Trainers for grip
- An expert to help you, as even professional rock climbers never climb alone

Stick a photo of you rock climbing here:

TOP TIP

Rocks can be slippery, especially if wet. Build up slowly before venturing too high and soon you'll be climbing Bond-style. This isn't the kind of thing you do everyday, so join a class or go to an event. Visit the 50 things website to find out more.

How many metres do you think you climbed overall? Write it here so you can try and beat it next time round.

Date completed: Day _____ Month _____ Year _____

47. Cook on a campfire

There's no kitchen in the great outdoors but you don't have to miss dinner.

What you need:

- A campfire
- Your chosen ingredients
- Cooking equipment, such as skewers for your marshmallows, a pot for your beans or a pan for your bangers
- A grown-up to check you don't spoil dinner

Write a recipe for something that you cooked on the campfire:

TOP TIP

This is not the time for a Sunday roast with all the trimmings. Keep it simple at first with food that cooks quickly and easily. Sausages, soups or beans all work well.

Date completed: Day _____ Month _____ Year _____

48. Learn to ride a horse

Learn to ride a horse like a proper cowboy.

What you need:

- An activity centre or stables where you can ride
- A grown-up to instruct you
- A riding hat, comfortable (but not baggy) clothes and boots

TOP TIP

Remember to listen very carefully to your instructor, so that you can learn to ride your horse safely.

Stick a photo of you riding a horse here:

What would your horse's racing name be? Write it here:

Date completed: Day _____ Month _____ Year _____

49. Find a geocache

With over a million in the world, there must be one around here somewhere...

What you need:

– A smartphone or handheld GPS

Draw what was inside
your geocache:

TOP TIP

Get involved and join a
geocache community
online. The largest is
geocaching.com

What would you leave inside a
geocache for someone else to
find? Write a list in this box:

Date completed: Day _____ Month _____ Year _____

50. Canoe down a river

See the world from a duck's point of view.

What you need:

– A canoe
– Paddles
– A life jacket
– A river
– Expert advice and supervision

Did you see any wildlife when you were canoeing? Draw what you saw in the space below:

TOP TIP

Going round and round in circles can get a bit boring. Paddle evenly on both sides to go in a straight line and actually get somewhere. This isn't the kind of thing you do everyday – join a class or go to an event.
Visit the 50 things website to find out more.

Look out for dragonflies and water birds, like herons and moorhens. You might even spot a little egret too!

Date completed: Day _____ Month _____ Year _____

10 best things to do

As voted for by you

1

Play in the snow

(page 30)

DID YOU KNOW?

Snow is made from lots of tiny ice crystals, known as snowflakes. No two flakes are exactly the same shape.

Canoe down a river

(page 71)

(page 71)

DID YOU KNOW?

The world's oldest boat is a canoe which was discovered in Holland. It is thought to be almost 10,000 years old!

2

3

Learn to ride a horse

(page 69)

DID YOU KNOW?

Horses can sleep
standing up or
lying down.

Camp out in the wild

(page 16)

DID YOU KNOW?

Being in a tent might mean you hear the dawn chorus, when songbirds sing at the start of a new day.

4

Build a den

(page 17)

DID YOU KNOW?

As your old den rots, it will be eaten by fungi, insects and other invertibrates – all of which love rotting wood.

6 Cook on a campfire (page 68)

DID YOU KNOW?

Jacket potatoes are easy to cook, as they can be wrapped in foil. You can make a great campfire meal just with a jacket potato and some baked beans.

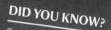

DID YOU KNOW?

Some people believe that the seventh wave is always bigger than the others. Scientists aren't so sure, but see what you think!

Jump over waves

(page 35)

8

Try rock climbing

(page 67)

DID YOU KNOW?

The youngest ever person to climb Mount Everest was only 13!

9

Go swimming in the sea

(page 63)

DID YOU KNOW?

Waves are made by the wind, which is powered by the sun. Air rises as the sun heats it, and cold air rushes in behind, creating the wind.

Build a raft

(page 64)

(page 64)

10

DID YOU KNOW?

If you're building a raft you'll need to learn some good knots to tie everything together, whether it's a big raft you can ride on or a toy one.

50 best places

Here are just some of the best places across the country to do each of the 50 things. Find somewhere near you at nationaltrust.org.uk/50things

 1. Climb a tree

Wallington
Northumberland

 2. Roll down a really big hill

Croome
Worcestershire

 3. Camp out in the wild

Gibside
Tyne & Wear

 4. Build a den

Lyme Park, House and Garden
Cheshire

 5. Skim a stone

Fell Foot Park
Cumbria

 6. Run around in the rain

Finch Foundry
Devon

 7. Fly a kite

Dunstable Downs
Bedfordshire

 8. Catch a fish with a net

Parke
Devon

 9. Eat an apple straight from a tree

Llanerchaeron
Ceredigion

 10. Play conkers

Osterley Park and House
London

 11. Go on a really long bike ride

Wimpole Estate
Cambridgeshire

 12. Make a trail with sticks

Longshaw and Eastern Moors
Derbyshire

13. Make a mud pie

Moseley Old Hall
Staffordshire

14. Dam a stream

Prior Park Landscape Garden
Somerset

15. Play in the snow

Bodiam Castle
Sussex

16. Make a daisy chain

Lacock Abbey
Wiltshire

17. Set up a snail race

Lyveden New Bield
Northamptonshire

18. Create some wild art

Sheringham Park
Norfolk

19. Play pooh sticks
Mottisfont
Hampshire

20. Jump over waves

Compton Bay and Downs
Isle of Wight

21. Pick blackberries growing in the wild

Castle Ward
County Down

22. Explore inside a tree

Hatfield Forest
Hertfordshire

23. Visit a farm

Cuckmere Valley
Sussex

24. Go on a walk barefoot

Strumble Head to Cardigan
Pembrokeshire

25. Make a grass trumpet

Hare Hill
Cheshire

26. Hunt for fossils and bones

Birling Gap and the Seven Sisters
Sussex

27. Go star gazing

Tyntesfield
Somerset

28. Climb a huge hill

Ashridge Estate
Hertfordshire

29. Explore a cave

Yorkshire Dales: Upper Wharfedale
Yorkshire

30. Hold a scary beast

Clumber Park
Nottinghamshire

31. Hunt for bugs

Hardcastle Crags
Yorkshire

32. Find some frogspawn

Springhill
County Londonderry

33. Catch a falling leaf

Rowallane Garden
County Down

34. Track wild animals

Castle Drogo
Devon

35. Discover what's in a pond

Florence Court
County Fermanagh

36. Make a home for a wild animal

Fountains Abbey and Studley Royal
Yorkshire

37. Check out the crazy creatures in a rock pool

South Milton Sands
Devon

38. Bring up a butterfly

Anglesey Abbey,
Cambridgeshire

39. Catch a crab

Plas Newydd
Gwynedd

40. Go on a nature walk at night

Nostell Priory
Yorkshire

41. Plant it, grow it, eat it

Tredegar House
Newport

42. Go swimming in the sea

Llŷn Peninsula
Gwynedd

43. Build a raft

Borrowdale
Cumbria

44. Go bird watching

Kingston Lacy
Dorset

45. Find your way with a map and compass

Chartwell
Kent

46. Try rock climbing

Brimham Rocks
Yorkshire

47. Cook on a campfire

Stackpole
Pembrokeshire

48. Learn to ride a horse

Clandon Park
Surrey

49. Find a geocache

Sizergh
Cumbria

50. Canoe down a river

Brancaster Millennium Activity Centre
Norfolk

Spring

32. Find some frogspawn

> *It's amazing finding frogs' eggs in a pond and to think they will grow into tadpoles and then into frogs!*

Recommended by Leon, aged 5, East Sussex

44. Go bird watching

> *Birds are amazing animals and you might spot really rare ones*

Recommended by Olivia, aged 9, Yorkshire

31. Hunt for bugs

" *Some people are scared of creepy crawlies but they mean us no harm* "

Recommended by Natalie, aged 11, Midlothian

28. Climb a huge hill

" *Because everyone can do it if they try. Climbing a hill is a good thing to do to keep you fit and the views you get when you are at the top are amazing!* "

Recommended by Katy, aged 9, Staffordshire

41. Plant it, grow it, eat it

" *I really like gardening and growing, you have fun getting mucky* "

Recommended by Katie, aged 10, Hampshire

3. Camp out in the wild

It will let you hear what happens at night out in nature!

Recommended by Lily, aged 8, West Sussex

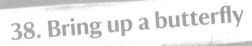

38. Bring up a butterfly

It's really adventurous and gives you a chance to discover the life of a butterfly

Recommended by Chloe, aged 11, Northumberland

2. Roll down a really big hill

It is the BEST fun and I have done it with so many friends and we have all loved it

Recommended by LouLou, aged 11, Lincolnshire

39. Catch a crab

It's a really fun thing to do at the beach. You could have medals for the winners, gold is the one with the biggest crab. Remember to put the crabs back in the sea afterwards

Recommended by Olivia, aged 9, Devon

42. Go swimming in the sea

It isn't hard to do and it's different to swimming in a swimming pool

Recommended by Eloise, aged 9, Essex

14. Dam a stream

It is fun to work out where the water is getting through and find ways to block it off

Recommended by Alice, aged 8, Oxfordshire

46. Try rock climbing

Rock climbing should be included because it's fabulous

Recommended by Lucy, aged 10, Merseyside

Autumn

9. Eat an apple straight from a tree

I have an orchard in my front garden and this is one of my most favourite things to do

Recommended by Kevin, aged 5, County Down

30. Hold a scary beast

I like to count how many legs it's got!

Recommended by Emily, aged 4, London

49. Find a geocache

It turns a walk into an adventure and you have to watch out for muggles (who are not geocachers) so it is secret. I have to work out puzzles and write down what I have found, and adults enjoy it too

Recommended by James, aged 5, Yorkshire

21. Pick blackberries growing in the wild

Because blackberries are tasty and easy to find, and it is fun cooking with them

Recommended by Zoë, aged 9, Staffordshire

40. Go on a nature walk at night

I did it when it was my 4th birthday with my Mum, Dad and brother. We walked in some fields and found a badger track, saw some rabbits and looked for the moon. The best bits were seeing the bats flying and looking at the stars.

Recommended by Ned, aged 4, Gloucestershire

10. Play conkers

Because it's a fun game you can enjoy, and you can decorate your conkers, too
Recommended by Tiana, aged 11, Surrey

12. Make a trail with sticks

I did this with my Mummy, Daddy and brother and it was really fun using sticks as arrows to show the way

Recommended by Joshua, aged 8, London

93

34. Track wild animals

You can go for long walks in woods or forests looking for animal tracks to follow and hopefully see animals close up

Recommended by Daniel, aged 6, London

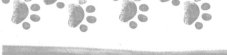

22. Explore inside a tree

Looking inside a tree is fun. I climbed inside and hid from my Mum. Inside one of the trees the pattern looked like a face. It was a bit scary. I laughed when my Mum found me. I had a magnifying glass so I could look for mini beasts. The trees were really old

Recommended by Wilf, aged 5, Gloucestershire

15. Play in the snow

It's magical

Recommended by Lily, aged 8, West Sussex

27. Go star gazing

When I was camping me and my Mum were looking at the stars and I saw the Plough and Orion's Belt. I have asked for an astronomy book for my birthday so that I can look for more. I think other children would like it too

Recommended by Amy, aged 9, Oxfordshire

45. Find your way with a map and compass

It is a really fun activity and adults can join in too

Recommended by Ben, aged 11, Cleveland

26. Hunt for fossils and bones

It's fun going on a walk and looking for fossils and very exciting if you find one

Recommended by Rebecca, aged 11, Shropshire